*For my parents,*
*thank you for always encouraging*
*me to follow my dreams.*

Amy's Dreaming Adventures

The Enchanted Forest

Chrissy Metge

Amy loves fantasy, fairies and more,
But only in dreams can Amy explore.

So into her bed Amy jumps every night
With Snowy her owl who helps her take flight.

Almost as soon as she lays down her head,
Amy and Snowy fly far from her bed.

Off into dreamworlds the pair will soar -
Tonight with a fairytale forest in store!

"Hello everyone!" Amy gleefully grins.
The sprites are all singing! The journey begins!

The fairies all join in their happiest song.
They sing and they sing and they sing all night long.

Pouncing from pad to pad to pad,
A queue of croakers follow their dad:
A family of frogs in a lily pad pond,
Leaping to meet this girl from beyond.

The trolls of the forest climb up from below.
(They live in the tunnels beneath, you know.)

They greet the pair with a joyful shout!
The trolls even smile! (They usually pout.)

Even the grassy old turtle comes out
            To see what all the fuss is about.

He stays for a moment, then turns and withdraws.
        (A turtle, you see, is not one for applause.)

Then colorful parrots from high in the trees
Swoop down and swirl like a rainbow breeze.

Violet! Blue! Yellow, orange red!
They gather up garlands and crown
Amy's head.

The elves bring Amy a beautiful dress.
They bow and name Amy an elven princess!

"Princess?" Snowy asks.
"They think that's what you are?

If you're a princess, then we must have flown far!"

"Not far enough!" Amy says with a wink.
"This forest is holding more secrets, I think!"

Then deeper they go, inside Amy's dream,
'Til Amy and Snowy discover a stream.

"This is the place!" Amy whispers a smile.
They hide by a tree and they wait for a while.

There's one thing she'd dreamed of, since she
was born: To meet a real live unicorn.

And then it appears: Pink, silver, gold.
The most beautiful sight a girl could
behold. It sips from the stream and
peeks Amy's eye. It neighs and it
whinnies a mini goodbye.

Amy knew it was time to go.
The time always comes,
whether fast, whether slow.

Back to her bed the travelers flew.
Was it real? Just a dream? Amy knows... Do you?


THE END.

**Chrissy Metge**

With an extensive background and love of animation it seemed
a natural progression to add childrens' author to her list of talents.
As a new mother, one of her most favourite things is getting to see
all the little things in life, all over again.

*The Enchanted Forest* is the first book in the series
of Amy's Dreaming Adventures.

**Chrissy the Author has other great titles available:**
**www.ducklingpublishing.com**

www.ingramcontent.com/pod-product-compliance
Lightning Source LLC
Chambersburg PA
CBHW080507030726
47592CB00011B/3285